Love
Life
Loss

and a little bit
of hope

Also by Chief R. Stacey Laforme

Living in the Tall Grass
Poems of Reconciliation

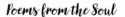

Poems from the Soul

Love
Life
Loss

and a little bit
of hope

Chief R. Stacey Laforme

Foreword by Kevin Hearn

Afterword by Kate Laforme

DURVILE &
UpRoute

Calgary, Alberta, Canada

DURVILE.COM

UpRoute Imprint of Durvile Publications Ltd.
Calgary, Alberta, Canada
www.durvile.com

Library and Archives Cataloging in Publications Data

LOVE LIFE LOSS
and a little bit of hope

Laforme, Chief R. Stacey; Author
Hearn, Kevin; Foreword
Laforme, Kate; Afterword
Gibbon, Samantha; Illustrator

1. First Nations | 2. Anishinaabe | 3. Poetry
4. Truth and Reconciliation | 5. Indigenous Peoples

The UpRoute "Spirit of Nature" Series

Series Editors, Raymond Yakeleya and Lorene Shyba
Issued in print and electronic formats
ISBN: 978-1-990735-43-1 (pbk); 978-1-990735-52-3 (e-pub)
978-1-990735-51-6 (audiobook)

Front cover design, Samantha Gibbon | Book design, Lorene Shyba
Thank you Brianna Haydu for proofreading.

Durvile Publications acknowledges financial support for book development and production
from the Government of Canada through Canadian Heritage, Canada Book Fund
and the Government of Alberta, Alberta Media Fund.

The lands where our studios stand are a part of the ancient homeland and traditional territory of
many Indigenous Nations, as places of hunting, travel, trade, and healing. The Treaty 7 Peoples of
Southern Alberta include the Siksika, Piikani, and Kainai of the Niisitapi (Blackfoot) Confederacy;
the Dene Tsuut'ina; and the Chiniki, Bearspaw, and Wesley Stoney Nakoda First Nations. We also
acknowledge the homeland of the Métis Nation of Alberta. We honour the Nations and Peoples, as
well as the land. We commit to serving the needs of Indigenous Peoples today and into the future.

Dedication

I dedicate this book to everyone who has lost someone special. To everyone who struggles with that loss, that pain, and who tries to find the sun behind the clouds.

Contents

>⸙<

Foreword
Allyship

⤙⤚

Back in 2016, I had the honour of helping Gord Downie bring his "Secret Path" record to the live stage. Before the first concert in Ottawa, Gord, along with me and the rest of the Secret Path band, were invited to participate in a healing ceremony with residential school survivors. The experience deeply affected me—in fact, it changed my life. I embraced the idea of allyship. I made a personal commitment to learn more, and do more. The journey has been difficult, humbling, and rewarding.

I believe that anyone who sets out on this path will soon meet friends and teachers along the way. Giima Stacey Laforme has been one of my great teachers. His lessons are available to all who read his poems, which are rich in wisdom and gracefully articulated in down-to-earth language that gets right to the heart of the matter.

In 2019, I helped the Downie and Wenjak families restage The Secret Path at Massey Hall. This time, Gord's songs would be sung by an amazing lineup of artists, both Indigenous and non-Indigenous, including Tanya Tagaq, William Prince, Lori Blondeau, and members of The Tragically Hip.

In a typical concert, before the music begins, it's customary to have welcoming and informative speeches from individuals affiliated with the Gord Downie & Chanie Wenjack Fund (DWF). However, for the upcoming performance, I aimed to create a transition that would seamlessly guide the audience from the speeches to the musical experience. I envisioned a spoken word piece infused with creative expression, designed to encapsulate the essence and purpose of the event. Ideally, it would eloquently convey the significance of the gathering.

Through my work with the DWF, I had become friends with Chief Perry Bellegarde, former National Chief of the Assembly of First Nations (AFN), and his wife Valerie (Galley) Bellegarde. I asked them if they knew of any Indigenous poets or writers who might be interested in participating in this bridge building between the speeches and the music. They immediately recommended Chief Stacey Laforme.

I ordered Chief Stacey's book *Living in the Tall Grass: Poems of Reconciliation*. A few days later, I sat down and read it from cover to cover. Then, at the Massey Hall event, Stacey's live reading of his powerful poem "Prayer" set the perfect tone for the heartfelt performances that were to follow. Chief Stacey and I have continued to collaborate and perform together since then.

In his new book *Love Life Loss and a little bit of hope*, Stacey's graceful way of addressing some of the deepest human experiences is even more powerful and inspiring. Here, he presents thought-provoking and healing meditations on this journey of life. He writes from experience, from his perspective as a son, father, husband, community leader, but most of all as a human being. In other poems, he may suddenly give voice to a grandmother, a tree, or a bison.

In the poem "Walk With Me" he writes:

> See the world as I see the world.
> Understand the world
> as I understand it.
> Let us learn from each other ...

He invites us to walk with him, and to see the world as he sees it. Not only is this an invitation we should accept, but it is also a beautiful and generous gift.

—*Kevin Hearn*
Musician, and member of the band
Barenaked Ladies
2024

Prologue
Storytelling

>—()—<

I TELL STORIES USING POETRY. A moment in time written from the perspective of the subject of the poem. They are not all written in first person, but enough so that you may notice.

It was my intent to write a book that chronicled my life to this point.

It has been an interesting journey through violence and abuse, homelessness and despair. Yet it has also been a life of accomplishment.

I intended to tell you my story using poetry and prose to get to this moment in time. Yet when I sat down to write this tale. I realized that a lot of the poems I wrote would not be included in that story, as they were written during the pandemic, or they were written about the uncovering of our children on sites at residential schools. They dealt with love, life, loss, and hope, and I realized this is the story I want to share.

I was again envisioning chapters and sections similar to my other book *Living in the Tall Grass,* but I soon realized that it wasn't going to be possible. You see love, life, loss, and hope are a part of not just one story but almost every story.

I think it is important to understand and share some of those moments with each other, so we can begin to heal. So that we do not lose faith in the world that surrounds us.

So, each of us can be reminded that it is our responsibility to try and make the world a little better for our children and their children.

Every poem I write, every story I tell, I live through. I experience the moments and the emotions that go along with the story, and I want my readers to experience it as well and the only way to do that is to leave a little something of yourself behind.

Usually, I state that once the poem/story is over it no longer owns me, or I no longer own it. This book and the stories within may stay with me forever.

— *Giima R. Stacey Laforme, 2024*

Imagination

We lose touch with our inner magic

Our imagination was the catalyst for
so many of our adventures as a child

Adventures that allowed us to escape
and become anything or anybody

Strange we seem to let
that imagination slip away

Some would say we refocus it
on practical things

Things in life that matter

But this magic is something
we should hold onto

Because it does matter

It reminds us of grand adventures,
it reminds us of hope

And in these magic moments we matter

We remember that we are heroes, adventurers

Maybe only in our owns stories, maybe only
for moments, but we are heroes

And that is so important in the day after day
routine that becomes our lives

I wish I still had the imagination to let my
mind take me on an adventure

But though I still collect action figures and
toys, they mostly stay on the shelf
or in the box

No more dragons for me to slay or
supervillains to conquer

I remember those journeys, those adventures,
I miss them, but I cannot relive them

The magic or the imagination if you wish
has left me

I have searched inside for it but though I may
glimpse it, it is not attainable

I remember when every cloud
was its own story

I will not give up, I will look to the heavens,
I will examine those clouds

And I will dream and soar

And once again for a moment

I will be the most important thing
in my life.

Common Ground

Everyone hears something of themselves in
this poem and that teaches us that
no matter how far apart we may seem,
we are never so far that we cannot
find common ground.

No one thing can define us
For we are complex creatures,
dreamed in the mind of the Creator

We laugh when we should cry
We cry when we should laugh
We joke when in pain

We smile because tears could consume us
We love unconditionally and totally

We understand that family should come first
Yet family is not defined solely by blood

We are quick to anger, yet no one forgives faster
We are loyal and we are strong

When we commit, we are unwavering
We have survived much, but do not mistake
adaptation for resignation

You will always see us, for we will always be here
Standing for what we believe in,
standing beside each other
Doing what is right for our children, our future
We remember our obligation
to our Mother the Earth

And we remember our place upon her
We are a proud people and honorable people

We do not always do right, for we are human
And prone to the follies of humanity

Yet we strive to be better, to make each other better
To make the world a better place for the children
I know the Creator smiles upon us,
no matter where we are, or what we do

For the love of a child is unconditional
No matter where life takes you, walk proud.

Who Am I

Who am I, where do I belong?
It is a question that all seek to answer

Some people will try and tell you
who you are or who you are not
They will tell you that
you do or do not belong

Never listen to them,
for who you are is always here
In your breast where your spirit lives
Your heart and spirit
remember even if your mind forgets

We may lose our way
We may need to seek others to help guide us

But inside,
sometimes deep inside, there is the answer
It sometimes takes language or culture
to guide us

It sometimes takes sport or learning
for there is no one way
Yet once we understand and come
to realize who we are

We come to understand that we
belong anywhere and everywhere

Never let another determine who you are,
or tell you where you belong

You know your worth, your value
You were dreamed in the mind of the Creator

The Creator dreamed of
the most beautiful creature he could imagine
Then he made you

You know this
Your mind just needs to listen to your heart

And remember
Who you are and where you belong...
Everywhere.

Souls

Some souls are confined by the
boundaries of this world

Their prison is not walls of steel and stone
but flesh and bone

They do not belong chained to the physical

And so, the flesh, although
pleasurable and beautiful offering
moments of wonder, are not enough

They know not why they struggle

While others embrace
the wonders of this existence

They try so hard to fit,
to find that purpose, that reason

Some seek the passion of violence
or the quiet of a solitary life

Some seek love and cling desperately to it
wishing to find a path to peace
but it seldom works

Some souls are born beyond the life,
the rest of us must live

Some souls come to this world
prepared for the next

And whether they manage a day
or a hundred years

It is a life of struggle, a challenging journey

And when they leave us, we will cry
and despair

Because we know how special this soul

Still we must smile at least once in a while
for they are finally free.

Gifts

I have looked into the eyes of pain

I have held a hand as the last breath escaped

I have struggled to find a reason

I have turned away more than once

Yet I am compelled to return

I have not chosen these moments

These moments have chosen me

I am strength, I am courage,
I am love, I am trust

The way that has been chosen is not easy,
at times it is the hardest

I have been asked how? Why?

My answer is simple and,
to me, powerful

I ... Do ... Good.

Baamaapii

In our language, we have no word for goodbye.
We say baamaapii kaawaagamiin,
which means, "I will see you again, later."

I thought the following poem was a perfect use of
that phrase, so that has become the title of the poem,
shortened to mean I will see you again. It was
originally written for my Cousin Darla.

The world got a little dimmer
The heavens a little brighter

We are grateful for the gift of you
For the time you spent among us

You touched so many lives
So forgive us our tears as we seek
understanding

Rest assured that yours will be loved
and embraced
We will remember you

The good, the bad, the silly, the sad,
the strong and the stubborn
We will lift our heads and raise our eyes   →

We will honour you by our words
and our actions

But not today, for the hurt is too fresh
and the grief too new

Today we will share our pain
and our tears

Tomorrow will be soon enough
for us to be strong

You are the sum of everything you did, every
life you touched

The glue that held things in place,
the hand that helped when needed

The smile that said it will be okay,
the kiss that wiped away the pain

Your beauteous smile was only matched
by your heart and spirit

We know you do not wish to leave
this pain in your wake

That you would have strong words
for all of us

About need and obligation,
about the future

Do not fear, we will come together
and we will do you proud

Forgive us our moments of sorrow

For you cannot understand just how much
you mean to all of us

Just as when the sun rises,
it does not understand

The warmth, the life, the love that it gives

We know this is not goodbye

That your spirit is eternal
and your love forever

Journey well/Baamaapii

Old Friend

I sometimes notice people stare
Should I be flattered or suspicious?
There was a time,
when someone looked at me
I would look back and smile
I do not anymore;
still I wonder what, why do they look
And it isn't until I glance in a mirror
that I realize
I have become so used to tears
That sometimes I forget to wipe them away

I do not know if you look out of sympathy,
commiseration or just curiosity
I will acknowledge you
if I have the strength
Yet think nothing of it, if I do not
Because hurt and pain take energy
If you would cheer me or reach out,
do not, it is not necessary
The pain has become an old friend to me
there in the morning, the evening

Sometimes even visiting in my dreams
It has become a part of me for I cannot lose
the pain without losing the memories
And those I would keep

Someday the tears may dry
and the pain retreat
And I may again meet you with a smile
However, it will come, if it comes
In its own time
Nothing you do or say can change that

I know you cannot help but look
Its okay, to this, I have become accustomed
If you would help me,
just whisper a quiet prayer
And remember never to judge
For you may never know the cause
Of the pain you witness
But be assured, all tears are not equal.

I must explain a little of the next three poems.
I have friends and allies in a place called
Oakville, Ontario, and they requested a poem
on allyship. I, of course, said yes.

As I began, I realized that I had already
written something that would fit well
It was a story called "Walk with Me."

As I struggled to understand how I could
incorporate that into the poem of allyship, I
remembered another poem I had completed for
the opening of the CBC Olympics, which was
titled "I Promise."

"I Promise" has been altered slightly, as I had
the opportunity to perform it with
Kevin Hearn from Barenaked Ladies and
Josh Finnelson from Skydiggers. I added a
line to the original poem so we had equal
lines to recite.

I believe both poems stand well on their
own and convey their own message but the
pieces fit extremely well together once I wrote
another poem to connect them.

Walk with Me

Take my hand
Face this world with me

See the world as I see the world
Understand the world as I understand it

Let us learn from each other, of each other
Laugh with me, cry with me

Fight for me, fight with me
Pray with me, pray for me

Face this world with me
Let us walk together

Let us rejoice in the light
Or be by my side
when the dark claims me

Whatever tomorrow may bring
Let us walk together

Let us face it side by side
The first step is to know me
Remember no one travels this world alone.

I Promise

We live in a world that has such beauty
Yet the beauty is overshadowed
Even our Mother the Earth, cries
We are losing any sense of connection
To our planet, to each other
Our future is no longer promised

It was not supposed to be this way
We were promised love, happiness
and safety when we came to this world
Yet it seems promises no longer possess
the weight they once did
No longer are they born in the heart
and formed in the soul
But are merely words of convenience
that flow easily from un-considering lips
We were promised!

As each promise fell, so too did we
But we still need them,
never has it been more apparent
We need to reclaim the promise that we were
all born into, that we have a right to

Stand with me, take my hand, let us remember, and
let truth emerge from the heart, the spirit

A commitment that shall not break, nor wither
with age, but only grow stronger in time

Let us build on old promises and heal wounds

I promise, to be better, to do better

I promise, to love, honour and care for
our Mother the Earth

I promise, to ensure our children grow up and
do not live under the shadow of violence

I promise to embrace the things in life
that make you and I different

I promise that I will love you, even though
I may not know you

I shall not forget the past nor broken promises,
but neither shall I dwell there

I embrace this moment of truth and hope

I will carry this ideal, this dream,
this reality into our future

This is a truth that we can stand on, build on,

Before the Creator, in front of the world,
from my heart and soul

All this ...

I Promise.

Nii Jii

I am not a cause
I am not absolution
Yes, there is a wrong to right
A history to correct
But I am not a thing of pity
Nor am I a pillar of virtue
I am a part of this world
That makes us a part of each other

Walk with me, take my hand
See the world as I see the world
Understand as I understand
Let us learn from each other, of each other
Laugh with me, cry with me
Fight for me, fight with me
Pray with me, pray for me
Face this world with me
Let us walk side by side
Let us rejoice in the light
Or be there when the dark claims me
Whatever tomorrow may bring

Let us walk together
Let us face it side by side

The first step is to know me
Allies, friends? Perhaps
My allies don't cheer from their stools
They do not shake my hand and forget me
Friends don't stand aside,
when I stand up for what's right
My allies do not view the colour of my skin
They must see past this to my heart
Allyship is not an end, it is a beginning
An understanding that must welcome all
A voice for the future, for our people,
for our children, for our planet
We must raise consciousness and awaken others

This is a journey, a challenge
At its core it is about understanding, uniting,
it is about love
Stand with me, take my hand
Let truth emerge from the heart and spirit
A commitment that shall not break
nor wither with age   →

But only grow stronger in time

Let us build on our promise, heal wounds
and change our world

I promise to be better, to do better

I promise to love honour and care for
our Mother the Earth

I promise to protect the land, the water,
the sky and all things under, on and above

I promise to ensure our children grow up
and do not live under the shadow of violence

I promise to embrace the things in life
that make you and I different

I promise that I will love you even though
I may not know you

All this in front of the world, from
my heart and soul, in front of the Creator

I promise

Now we begin

My friend, my ally.

Anger/Rage

I am angry, not in your face

Jump up and down angry

I am deep in my bones angry

The stolen children

Murdered and missing women

The injustice of systems that do not know us
or care to know us

I feel the pain of my ancestors

It grows and grows, I add mine atop theirs
and I fear for the children to come

How much helplessness
and anger will they carry?

I have to remind myself that I am not angry
with the person who forgot to signal

Or the grocery clerk who just cannot get it right

Nor am I necessarily angry with you,
who sits across from me   →

I am angry for generation
upon generation of subjugation

That is an anger that cannot be quantified

I am not the only one,
my people are not the only ones

This is an affliction upon this country,
upon this planet

When you look around and say what
the hell is wrong with this world

make sure it's not you

We must begin to understand where
the pain and anger originates

So that we can begin to heal.

My Wish

My wish is to see you stand as one
To support each other through
the good and the bad

Do not let jealousy or past issues cloud your reason
Do not let small-mindedness stop you
Do not let loss and grief overwhelm you

It is so easy to be divided by pain and hurt
Yet it is the time to stand together
To love one another

Faced with horror
Do not become a part of it
Rather rise above it
with the strength of your ancestors

Let the children see you as you wish to be seen
Stand in the light in the darkest moment
And you will leave a legacy beyond wealth or power

You will leave a world full of hope
And hope is the brightest star
And our best possible future.

Hope

I sit waiting, with others who wait
Younger, older, some just babies

All are represented, there is no discrimination
Many fighting back tears, trying to be strong
for their loved ones

Trying to smile as their heart quietly breaks
Their pillows silent and sole witness, as the
grief overcomes them in the dark

They watch their loves at night
Not knowing what the future holds

If I am gone who will care for them
Who will love them, wipe their eyes,
dry their tears? Who will comfort them?

The dawn breaks and it is time to begin again
To smile and laugh, to pretend and hope

To come to this room
Or a room, somewhere else,
very much like this one

Resigned to the diagnosis
Yes, we all have it, we all know it

We will all fight, many of us will win
Still, some of us will not

For the winners life will go on, and we will
see hope in every sunrise
We will have won, but we will always fear the
unknown, what if it is not done

For the others,
the sunrises and sunsets will be few
And loved ones left behind must find a way
to cope, or at least live

For now, we all sit here as survivors

We all have hope
It is the one thing we cling hardest to

We come into this world crying but with
hope, we leave it quietly, but with hope
And we travel the road of life with hope.

Grief

I have seen so many people leave this place
I have grieved for each one

I have spoken words for many of them
I still hurt and cry at times for the pain
does not leave me

I wonder if something is wrong with me,
to be this raw and open
When I did not live with you,
I did not see you every day

Am I entitled to feel such hurt
Others are far closer and suffer so much

They have a right to their tears
Yet each loss weighs upon me

Every day something or someone
will remind me of you and yours
And I will feel the pain anew

It is as if I have lost family each time
I do not understand

I grieve for the Elders whose
wisdom and life has ended
I grieve for those taken
out of time by surprise

I grieve for the young who were just
awakening to this world
I shed a tear every day

Though I feel this pain
I know it is small in comparison to those
who love you, whose life you touched

I grieve every day for those gone
But I grieve most of all
for those left behind.

Prayer

We acknowledge the Creator,
the world around us and our place within

We thank you for the gifts we have been given

The gifts of this world, the insects, the animals,
the plants, the people

We are thankful for the breath of life,
the gift of spirit and energy

We ask that you shelter us and guide us in
these difficult and challenging times

We ask that you protect our Elders,
our knowledge keepers,

For they are the keepers of our wisdom,
our language and our past

We ask that you protect and guide our youth
for they seek direction

They were born to run and it is a time of stillness,
they are our hope, our future

We ask that you protect the women of the world

For they are the bringers of life and
the foundation upon which we build

We ask that you guide and protect our warriors
for they seek direction

They serve the will of the people and struggle
without that voice, that guidance

We ask that you calm and comfort our leaders;
we need their logic and their compassion

Yet they are overcome, with the pain
and hurt of the people

We ask that you shelter and guide
the other people of these lands

They are our brothers and sisters,
though at times they fail to see us

Without them, we cannot achieve the purpose
for what we were set upon this world

We understand that we must stand together,
that we must face this dark time in unity

We understand that there is a lesson here,
a lesson for all
and we pray that lesson is heard

We acknowledge the Creator,
the world around us and our place within.

Light Dark

I know you are beyond the pain and hurt
of this world and your spirit lives on

But I cry when I see those pictures/moments
of you with the children

I hurt when I see your smile
in a picture at an event

Remembering your humour, hearing your
laugh, all these things make my heart ache.

Some would say those are the moments
to treasure and I do

But I mourn the pure joy of those moments
with an understanding

That joy is now removed from the world
and we are less for it!

It is the loss of the sun/the light
you brought into our lives,

Not the dark that remains
that causes the pain

And they are two very different things!

Everything

I walk upon the river's edge
A turtle breaks the stillness of the water

I look and see my reflection cast back
I find a smile stretched across my face

I feel no worries, no concerns, no hurt and no pain
I am in no hurry, no rush, time has no meaning

I think about my family and my friends
It is the memories that have caused my smile

I see only the good times, feel only the love
I realize that it is more than seeing the eagle fly overhead

More than hearing the distant sound of a wolf
It is somehow all a part of me

I see, hear and feel all of it
Caress of the wind, a blade of grass, the sun on my face

All of it is part of me and I am a part of all
I have never felt so calm, so connected,
so much a part of everything

This is a good place
This is a beautiful, wondrous place

This is a place of peace
I love it here and someday so will you.

Sunshine

Hard to explain how it feels to leave all this behind
Especially on a beautiful sunny day
when the birds are singing
Always thought it would be a dark night
Or a long illness or a heart attack during twilight
Seems wrong somehow to pass away in the light
With the sun shining down on my face
Like many others I have made my peace
Still at the end, there is uncontrollable fear
Fear of the unknown, fear of leaving this world
Fear of leaving people behind
Fear of the pain and the tears I will cause
What will become of all of you?
Some of you still need me
Some will be sad they never said goodbye
or that I passed away alone
To be honest, in these moments
we are always alone regardless of the company
I wonder will I see those whom I loved
who passed before me?
There are many that I would speak with
Will I see you again somehow?

Will I hear your voice again?

I am a being of energy and energy can never
be destroyed, merely changed

Is there heaven or some such?

I suppose it does not matter

I mean either there is and I will be allowed to enjoy

Or I will be beyond such thoughts and aspirations

If only emptiness and nothingness await me

I shall be beyond pain and worries

So I suppose laugh or cry

Celebrate or mourn

Do as you need to do to get beyond
the loss of my presence

For in truth my death will be glorious or it will
mean little to nothing to me

It is your life that must be managed
and only you can do that

I take my leave; live, take what joy you are able

For one day you will walk this path

Some would say you will take wings and fly

Yet it is all unknown

So now, when you walk among the living

Is when you should take wing and fly

Baamiipii or Not.

Family

What makes a family?
Are a husband and a wife enough?

Do you need a house for a family?
Is marriage required?

Are a parent and a child family?
Is a gramma and an uncle family?
Are cousins family?

If only the children remain
are they still a family?
Even though they may
have children of their own.

Can your community be your family?
Can your people?
Seems to me that the only thing required
for family is love

Even death is not an obstacle to family
As long as you have love

Who do you love? That is your family
I do not know who you love,
or whom you consider family

I know there were and are many,
who consider you family
Who will miss seeing you
at all the events,
all the occasions

We will celebrate your life and smile
in your memory
For that is what families do.

Mother's Day

In every day, felt in every hug
Every bath, every breakfast, every kiss good night
Every trip to the store, every piece of advice
Every smile of joy and every tear from pain
Today we will say I love you, give you a hug
Maybe buy you a gift
Truth is, we have no need of gifts to see you smile
We see your smile in our minds every day
No need to hear you say I love you
For we hear it with every beat of our hearts
Although we wish it were not so
One day you will leave us
However, the love will always go on
We will hear it in every whisper of the wind
See it, feel it with every rise and fall of the sun
Know it with every memory we made
Today is about thanking you
But I think it is more about reminding us
To appreciate the greatest gift bestowed
The love between a child and a mother
Happy Mother's Day
Today, tomorrow and forever.

Hero Unsung

Many years I have
been abused and disrespected

In the service of my industry

Ridiculed and verbally abused

Too slow, am I deaf, am I dumb

The worse your day,
the worse you treat me

Yet I smile, oh sometimes I get upset

Shed a tear or react in kind to you

But it is I who pay for that outburst, not you

Circumstances have changed

Now you need me

You stand in line patiently for me

You are polite to me, respectful

I did not change, did you?

What will the future bring?

When the day comes, when you don't need me

Will you go back to the way it was?

Will I become an inconvenience again?

Will you and your children
still wave at me, thank me?

Tell me how much of a hero I am?

You know I could refuse and walk away

I will not more for me and mine then for you

But still some for you

Maybe more for you than you deserve

Today I am your hero

But what does tomorrow bring

We will see.

Magic

An expectant mother has magic all around her
The first time a child cries or crawls,
that is magic

The feeling of first love, magic
You can see it in the rising of the sun,
standing in a forest

Yet, we do not seem able to hold onto it
For most of us, the feelings go away,
even the ability to perceive it

Maybe it's routine, boredom,
maybe it's loss or just life
For whatever reason the magic leaves us

Maybe we are not meant to hold it
Just to see it and once in a while if we are lucky
to get caught up in it

However, there are a lucky few,
who hang on to it all their lives

Their eyes do not lose their sparkle
and their smile does not dim

The challenges that are in life
does not absorb their magic

It instead feeds it
so that they may share it with us

We do not perceive it as such,
for we no longer can

Yet it catches us up and provides
comfort, love and more

In the measure of time,
death claims them, as it will all of us

And we think that the specialness,
the magic, is lost

But it isn't, it seeped into our pores, our souls

It lives inside us, just as they do.

Pain

I am selfish

In my grief

Through my tears

I see only my pain

I forget the pain of others

And acceptable or not

It is not right, it is not correct

In our pain

We must not hurt others

They too grieve, and pushing them away

Or hurting them is wrong

Grief is not something to be attended
in quiet and solitude

For grief is born from love

And love must always be shared.

Justice

*The following poem was written for
Justice Harry LaForme upon his retirement.*

*I was asked to write something for him months before his
retirement but I did not. I waited until a couple days before the
retirement dinner and then I wrote it and framed it and gave it
to him in front of his family and friends.*

✖〜{}〜✖

So, I announce my retirement
What does it mean? I quit, I am done?

No, it means I am about to live as I choose
Even though I have faced life on my own terms

No job, no way of life was worth comprising who I am
I haven't always pleased people,
but that's not the road I chose

I am done this particular journey,
but I begin another
I will not do anything too different,
for this is what I love   →

It wasn't always love and it certainly wasn't
love at first sight

It was a job and a tough one

However, as time passed and
I immersed myself in this life

I felt the tug, the pull of Justice

She called me and I spent many
sleepless nights answering

I spent so many hours pushing
on the boundaries that make up the walls of Justice

The greatest part of this journey has been
serving my nation, my people

In an era when racism was rampant, I fought for the
rights of the Indigenous People

I was asked what is your greatest accomplishment

I could not answer, not because there are many
and each equally important

I could not answer because I have not
accomplished it yet, for I am not done

Whatever I do next, it will be related to the
pursuit of Justice and it will serve my people

Think of Justice as a tree and my journey
so far a branch on that tree

Wherever I go, whatever I do, I will stay on
that tree

I may choose a different branch

But I shall stay

And one day, when my time ends, I want you
to bury me beneath that tree

And my only marker to say,
'He upheld the law and always did
and always will search for truth, for Justice

Sometimes we do not get to choose
where we go in life

Sometimes life chooses for us.

The Truth of This Land

*This section was written after the discovery of the
unmarked graves of the children who attended
residential schools and who never came home.*

We knew there were those who never came home.

*We knew that our children were dead and buried
and no record kept.*

*Yet it is one thing to know something in your mind
and quite another to have the realization
break your heart.*

*The following poems were written in regards to
the uncovering of our children and when I say our
children I mean our children for they are
the children of this land,
of this country,
of this world.*

It started with 215 children,
now there are thousands!

The two poems that follow need a little introduction.

The first called "Reconciliation/215."
I wrote Reconciliation/215 the first night I heard about
it on television. I remember I was angry, I was sad, I
cried and I wrote Reconciliation/215.
215 was the number of children who were uncovered
on the residential site. It can be found on Youtube as
friends put music and a video to it.

The second poem is called "What if Canada Day/2021."
I had already sent a couple of videos out to different
cities that requested a video from me for Canada Day
before I heard of the uncovering of the children.
I called them and asked
if they would use this poem instead.

><><

Reconciliation/215

I sit here crying
I don't know why
I didn't know the children
I didn't know the parents
But I knew their spirit
I knew their love
I know their loss
I know their potential
And I am overwhelmed
By the pain and the hurt
The pain of the families and friends
The pain of an entire people
Unable to protect them, to help them
To comfort them, to love them
I did not know them
But the pain is so real, so personal
I feel it in my core, my heart, my spirit
I sit here crying and I am not ashamed

I will cry for them,

And the many others like them

I will cry for you, I will cry for me

I'll cry for what could have been

Then I will calm myself,

Smudge myself, offer prayers

And know they are at peace

In time I will tell their story

I will educate society

So their memory is not lost to this world

And when I am asked

What does reconciliation mean to me?

I will say, I want their lives back

I want them to live, to soar

I want to hear their laughter

See their smiles

Give me that

And I'll grant you reconciliation.

What if Canada Day/2021

This year you will not see any parades
You will see no fireworks light up the sky

This July 1 will be quiet and thoughtful
as we gather with family and friends

As we consider the legacy and
the future of this country

The truth is before us, there are no more excuses
to be made or accepted

And awful, unimaginable truth
has been confirmed

This land is built on the bones of Indigenous People
And the tears of their children

They wept for stolen children
As we hugged and loved ours

They grieved as their future died at a desk,
in a bed, at the hand of a stranger

We sent ours to school, to chores, kissed them
goodnight as we tucked them into bed

So, there can be no Canada Day this year
There can be no celebration

We will not have our Indigenous
brothers and sisters mourn
As we sing, dance and make merry

This is a moment in the life of this country
That will determine our future
We need to be united in this moment

To express our love and,
equally important, our support
For this is not just the Indigenous history,
it is our history

These are not just the Indigenous children;
they are all our children,
the children of this land
And we cannot celebrate
until we have justice for our children

We have answers for our people and we have
accountability for our future
We are with you today and always
What if?

Debwewin (Truth)

The uncovering of our children
is a big part of the story of this land

It is a glimpse into the atrocities of the past

It is an understanding that the earth
embraces the innocent

She could not help; she could only
bear witness to the tears
and terror of children

In the end, she could only do what she can do

And that is to embrace them and hold them

Until they are found
and returned to their families

She saw them lifeless and limp

She felt the shovels enter her body

She felt the young dumped into the holes

Silent witness and caretaker

This is not the first of the atrocities
she is witness to

Sadly, it will not be the last.

Orange Shirt Day

Removal of children from homes
Removal from nature
Removal from culture
Removal from language, customs and practice
Removal from everything they have ever known
Removal from love

I cannot think of the pain and horror
of those lost and those who survived
Without tears welling up,
without anger entering my heart
Tears are cleansing so we do not deny them
But we rise above the anger because your treatment
of us in the past cannot control us today
That was the intent of the residential school system
To control us, to take away from who we are

It did not work then and it will not work now
Today and every day we remember who we are
Today and every day we remember those stolen
Today and every day we remember
those who never returned
Today and every day we remember those who lived
through the residential school system
And those who live through it still.

Truth

Truth is not the absence of a lie

It is not a factual account of
an event or occurrence

Truth is not the things
we teach or describe

Truth is not the words we share

Truth is in the life we live.

What is Beauty

Everyone sees beauty
in so many different things

What is better? A sunset or a sunrise?

A child's laugh or a partner's smile?

Holding hands or making love?

A peaceful river, a raging torrent?

An eagle in motion or completely calm?

Dark clouds and a storm?

Cats, dogs, pets?

Yesterday, tomorrow?

We all see it so different

There is no right or wrong

Beauty is in everything.

Inspiration

Inspiration may be fleeting

Yet it never truly leaves

It exists buried in our subconscious

The trick is to answer when it calls

Making difficult change can survive a
moment of inspiration

But not a lifetime of commitment.

My Truth

What is my story?
What is my truth ?

I am a son, a father, a brother
My parents have passed, my brother is gone,
but still they are part of who I am

I have been a hero to some, a coward to others
The world to my wife and child

A leader, a follower, a wise man and a fool
I face all the demons that you face

I face all the pain of the past,
all the generational trauma
You may not see my hurt, for I choose not to let you

But never doubt it is there
It is there in the quiet of darkness

It is there in the brightness of day
It is there behind every smile
Every hug and every welcoming handshake

My demons have not overtaken me,
I am still here, unlike others
Whose personal demons have claimed them

Does this mean I win, I do not believe it is
something that can be won
It can only be survived, for I expect to wage
this battle all my mortal life

So, when I say my demons have not claimed me
Maybe it is proper to say
they have not, as of yet

I hope that small steps, small victories
May ease the pain of the next generation

Everything I accomplish in life
Will be because of and in spite of my demons
My story is your story, my truth is your truth
The only thing that distinguishes us,
is how we live it.

Thank You

At first, we knew only mom
Then we came to know family
But you are our first adventure
Our first moments of independence
First stranger, first friend
So important to our lives
to shaping who we will be tomorrow
It will not be easy
We will make you struggle
Maybe even cry
We will bond with you, we will love you
We will miss you and we will terrorize you
One day we will leave you
To go on to our next step
We will grow up
And begin families of our own
When you meet the grown me
I hope that we will remember each other
However, in case life makes me forget
I want to say thank you, for without you
I would not be the me that I will be.

Biindigin (Welcome)

In a time where disease isolates us
In a world where racism divides us
In this moment of chaos and confusion
This is a good place
This is a needed place
This is a place of equals
A place to stand or kneel side by side
To understand your
connection to our mother

To understand your connection
to each other

To understand who you are
and where you belong

Where all are welcome

Be at peace
Bindiigin.

Mortal

I love my children, I love my family, my friends
I love my life

Yet I have always felt the walls surround me

A sense of disconnectedness has always troubled me

I have always felt there is more just out of reach

Beyond the boundaries that I have built

And beyond the boundaries of my humanity

I die and I am free of flesh, my time complete

I soar, unencumbered by the frailties of humanity

Unencumbered by the limits of my mind

Connected to everything, everyone

Full to the brim with so much positive energy

A sense of completeness envelops me
a universal sense of belonging

Yet I feel you tug on me
your tears and your pain pull at me

And I am reminded of you and all that we had
all that I left undone

And I would come back if I could

I would give up all this new-found knowledge,
all this beauty, this belonging

To spare you one moment of pain
I would come back

Maybe that's why things are as they are,
why we do not get to choose the time of our passing

Why we are mortal and have limitations

Because if we had the choice we would
all come back, we would never leave

For even though we have earned our spot in the
heavens, none of us would accept it

Not because we fear the unknown,
but because of the love that is known

So, we are forced to let each other go

You may be angry that I am gone

But, I have had my time, I have earned my place

My love for you exists beyond
the humanity that once defined it.

From Love

This Christmas will be hard
As we listen to the music, exchanging gifts
Trying to smile through our heart aches

Loved ones have left this physical world
We think of them and we miss them
We struggle with a simple smile

Because smiling and laughing,
will always conjure a memory
Yet the loved ones, who have gone on,
do not wish us tears
They would understand
but it is not sorrow they seek

They need to know that those left behind,
will be all right
That our hearts can still sing
They want to see the smiles and hear the laughter

They want this for the little ones, for their family
and friends, for those they love
They need this for us and partly for them
For their peace and ours are forever entwined

I will do my best to make this holiday
sing and laugh
It's what he, she, and they would want
To know, that our grief
does not overshadow the joy

This will be challenging and if a tear fails me
I will look up, smile and continue to love
Celebrating the angels above us
and the ones still in our care

And you will know that in time,
we will be okay
We will think of you, we will miss you,
we will smile and we will cry
But you will know, it is done from love.

My Boy

On the day you were born I cried,
I was so happy to have my son

No one saw me but I did
I also grinned from ear to ear

You were the most perfect and
most beautiful child
I had ever seen

You spent your days in the crib
and your nights in my arms

You learned to walk, but never too far from me

You slept with me, ate with me,
grew in front of me

I was there for every new experience,
every bump and bruise

Every struggle, every nightmare, every tear

Too soon, you become a man, no longer my baby,
my child, at least in your mind

In mine you were, you are, and you will always be

As a man, you had challenges
that you would face alone

Challenges that you believed were yours to deal with

And I let you, I didn't want to, but I had to

We did not always agree, but we always had love
Oh, it was not talked about as much
as when you were a child

However, it was still apparent to me
and I hope to you
I thought we would have forever, all the time
in the world to deal with every issue

My greatest fear was how you would
handle my death
I hoped you would be able to cope
to go on without me

I suppose all parents worry about
leaving their children alone
We never want to cause pain or hurt for
someone we love, someone we created

And now the unthinkable has happened,
death has stolen you
It is ironic that now, I am left to deal with the pain
and the loss that I wished to spare you

This is not the way it is supposed to be, I struggle,
my mind refuses to accept this
I do not know what I am to do, where I am to go,
why I am still here   →

I keep expecting to see you laughing
and walking through the door

My mind knows, but my spirit tries
to protect me

You may not have been the man
I thought you would be

You may not even have been the man
you wanted to be

But you were nowhere near done

You had so much more to experience
to become the true you

You may not have been perfect,
but you were, you are, my son,
and that is enough

I love you, I miss you, and I always will

Until we meet again,
know that you shall forever live in my mind,
my heart and my soul

You may have left this world as a man

But to me you never stopped
being my beautiful baby boy.

What is Brave

Living a life pushed into shadow
For those who sit in the sun
Pushing against a door that is closed
Until that door opens
Forcing a superficial world to look deeper
To demand your place in line
When others try to push you out
To speak, to shout, to talk
When those perceived above quiet you
I am not sure what brave is, but I know it is needed
I know we are at a time when each voice matters
We can no longer be silent and shake our heads
nor nod our agreement
The world needs your voice, all our voices
No longer can we remain silent
No longer can we let only one perspective be heard
Time to use our voice
For those who can no longer and
for those who are yet to come
Time to speak
Time to be brave?

Nashville Dream

I share myself with the world
So I need the quiet downtime

You see! A singer, songwriter
Someone to make you laugh, at times cry

Someone to make you dance
You turn to music in joy and in solace

I create those moments for you
to enjoy, or to reflect
Then, I perform those moments and sometimes
it is at great personal cost

For words and lyrics are not plucked out of the air
They come from the soul, the spirit

And there is a cost to that

Sometimes I do not feel like singing, entertaining
mostly I do it for others, not for me

So, if in the quiet moments I stand apart

Or I prefer a game of chess to a party
You must understand I do not reject you
I embrace the solitude and quietness because I need it

Many "Performers" are just that

To the world, to the fans, we are an image
But if you were allowed to peak behind the curtain
you would see so much more

Do not mistake me, I love to sing,
to write, to perform
I would sing even if no one would listen
But I am more than the music

I have lived a life of love, loss and hope
Yes, we dream of stardom
We chase the energy and the experience
that goes along with it

We can appear changed but deep down
where it counts we remain
I hope you didn't mistake humble for arrogant
Or a performance for reality

Strip it all down and you will find the same spirit
That came into this world is the same spirit
who will leave it
To my fans I wish I had one more song to sing you
To my family
I wish I had one more hug to give you.

✄—{}—✄

Baamaapii Kaawaagiimin

I wrote this poem for a little girl named Kelsey
whose bravery and love shined.
I did not really know the family,
but I felt connected to them by the radiance of her soul.

I don't have to know you to love you!

✄—{}—✄

Angel

I had no wings

No halo had I

I did not sit in church

But I did believe

I love my family

I love my friends

I love people

I love myself

I lost my struggle

I did not give up

But I did not grow wings

I went into the earth; I went away

Yet I am never gone

For everyone who remembers me

Carries me inside their mind, in their heart

There was pain but it did not change me

I came into this world a beautiful soul

And that is exactly how I left it

I did change you

I made you feel so much love

Yes, you hurt, but you grew so much

And your heart was filled so full

And it was not just you

It was family, friends and even strangers

Am I an angel?

I do not know

But I know, I made you, all of you

Just a little bit closer.

Zaagi idiwin/leafde

When I first saw you

I noticed your hair, your smile,
and your bedroom eyes

However, it was your heart

That I fell in love with

Your sense of humour

Your personality

I am not perfect

You are not perfect

But somehow, sometimes

We are

We have loved, laughed and cried

Brought life to this world

Created a home

Became a part of each other

It has not always been easy

But it has always been worth it

I will hold your hand for as long
as the world will allow

And when the day comes that your hand,
does not rest in mine

I want you to know
the choice was not mine to make

For there is no place I would rather be

Then by your side, in your arms

Know that I will forever be
within smiling distance

Your handsome husband.

Unconditional

The strength of the earth is hers
to birth, to grow, to give life
The strength of the water is hers
to nurture, to care and if needed
to shed a million tears

I have known a mother, a grandmother,
a daughter, a sister, an aunt, a wife
I have seen her at her best and her worst

I have seen strength, I have seen power
and I have seen compassion
I have seen anger, rage, and I have seen love

I have seen tears and hurt that can break
I have seen falls, struggles, and witnessed
as she stood time and time again

I have seen failure and loss
but I have never seen her quit
Is it the connection to the land,
the water?

Or is it as simple as
the limitless love she carries?

I am not sure and I guess
it does not really matter

All I can do and say to the women in my life

Is to show my appreciation
and say thank you

Thank you for being the force
you were and are

Thank you all.

Mother

*If you read Living in the Tall Grass or any of my
other writings, you may notice I write by trying
to place myself in the heart and soul of others at
different moments of their lives.*

*When I was young, I always thought I was
intended to be some type of healer, because I always
had an affinity for those who needed help. It was a
gift, but I had no one to teach me how to use
and deal with my gift.*

*I was lucky, for though I did not understand how
to use my gift, I fell into poetry and storytelling
which allowed me to use the gift
I was born with in a different way.*

*I believe that all children are born with gifts/
abilities and it is so important to recognize and
encourage those gifts. Because without knowledge
and support some gifts can become burdens.*

*I never would imagine that I would take the
ability I have to connect with other lives and give
voice to nature, to trees, to the Earth herself.*

*I suppose it should not be a surprise for they too
need a voice, they need to be understood.
Perhaps now more than ever!*

*The first poem is about nature but it is also a story
of a difference-maker known as Grandmother
Josephine (Water Walker), who walked half the
circumference of the Earth to raise awareness of
the spirit of water. I only met her one time for a
few minutes. Years later, I heard she was sick and
so I sat down and wrote the following poem from
my interpretation of her perspective.*

*I debated sending it to her as I felt it was
arrogant of me to presume I could know her
this well, but eventually I decided to send it and
I am happy that I did.*

*She passed away a short time later but we had a
chance to chat about the poem
which I was told she loved.*

Walks Forever Woman

I have been called a hero, I have been called crazy
It does not matter what people say,
but do not doubt I have been called
I saw the anguish upon the water, the pain, the hurt
I sat in ceremony with tears streaming
I knew I must do something and so I asked
Walk grandmother, sing, dance, ceremony, but walk

So walk I did for the water, sometimes with others,
sometimes alone
I thought that once my first walk was done
I would rest, but again I was called
walk grandmother
So I walked and I walked and always upon
the end of the walk
I thought now I rest, but the call is not gone,
so I walk
This may be the final time my feet travel the earth
around the water
Upon my deathbed, they will say you have done
enough, rest
I will smile and nod, for them

Yet I know I will continue on this journey

For I still feel the call, I still hear the voice
walk grandmother

I sometimes wonder why no one hears
the voice of the water

Maybe no one who is alive today remembers

So I will walk and you may hear my voice, my drum

You may walk by my side, or you
may glimpse my passing

This is not a curse, this is a cause, an honour

I will walk for the spirit of the water

I will walk until duty is not forgotten

I will walk until you walk

For I have learned that the voice says walk
but it means lead

So I will walk until you hear and you answer

So stand grandmothers, grandfathers, parents,
children stand

For you must stand and you must stand together

Then you must walk, and I will walk beside you

For even as I pass I hear the words
walk grandmother walk.

The Red Oak

There is a beautiful tree in Toronto Ontario
that is 350 years old. It is a Red Oak tree and
it was due to be removed.

A lady named Edith George along with many
allies fought to save the tree and they were
successful. I was asked to write a poem for
the tree. I sat down and wrote a poem called
"Stand" which obviously was not the poem they
wanted but it is the story that wanted to be
told. Later, I wrote another poem simply called
"Tree" which was much more appropriate for
the original Red Oak story.

Stand

You call me beautiful, amazing
You argue to preserve my life
You will fight so that I may remain
Yet you only notice me because I have been
called to your attention
Were I among my own in a field
would you even see me
They were and are killed in the hundreds,
the thousands
Who defends them, do you?
They have just as much right to existence as I
The place I live does not make me special
The years that have passed do not make me special
The fact you have noticed me
does not make me special
I am special because I am special
Because we are all special
If you do not see this or understand this
Then leave me in peace, leave me to my fate
For I will not forsake all my relatives
For the love of myself
Or for the love of you.

Tree

I am young to this Earth, yet I am old to you

I have felt the years pass by
in silence and solitude

I have seen my kind vanish
and yours grow as ants upon a log

Some have called me beautiful and majestic

I cannot disagree

Even if I could, you would not know

I cannot speak to you,
for you do not know how to listen

I have experienced the joy of friendship and love

I have witnessed events that would make you weep

You cannot know, you cannot guess

The stories I have to tell
the stories that will never be told

I am lonely, and it is
a lonely that you cannot imagine

There was a time that we existed all across this land

And we talked and laughed in our way

Then they fell one by one and
I wept and whispered goodbye

I wonder, am I the only one left?
For I call and no one answers

Even your kind no longer visit and I miss you

They climbed and played and laughed

We loved the joy that we were a part of

However, that too is gone
and again I am alone

Time passes and once again
I call and this time, there is an answer

It is a youngling! Maybe I am not alone

Your kind come again,
to look, to admire and even to speak

Perhaps it is time
to be beautiful and majestic once again

At least for a while.

Home

Trees straining toward the sky

Water splashing on the shore

All around, Mother Earth
reclaims the mark of man

Our curse, our failing has been and is
that we forget the value,
the peace, the love of nature

Yet at one time all held the land in esteem

All knew her value because
she was always there
providing, nurturing

Yet as man moved away, he lost sight of nature,
he lost sight of her value

And because so much of man is part of the earth
and so much of the earth is a part of man

That as he moves away he forgets

He loses a small part of who he is

He does not notice, oh, he knows something
is missing but he does not remember

Yet all man need do is leave
the concrete and the steel

Walk to this spot, to nature and feel
at peace, relaxed, comforted, home

This is the connection, this the spirit of home
so close yet so far

The thing about home
is it is always there, always welcoming,
always waiting

And never truly gone.

Forest Rain

I have seen things made by man
that rival the Creator's hand

I have wondered at the Aurora Borealis,
the Grand Canyon and Niagara Falls
It appears that we try to
outdo the natural world

With constructions that reach for the stars
And composition that tug at the soul

We come close at times
But always come up short

Perhaps someday, perhaps not
Still beauty is beauty

Man-made or a creation of the divine
It still takes away the breath

And leaves one in awe
Yet never have I ever observed anything

In nature or man made
More beautiful than
Forest Rain.

Mother

Why do you hurt me
When I have nothing but love for you?

I have seen you crawl from the dark into the light
I have watched you learn to walk and then to fly

I have seen you squabble and fight
I have cheered for you and I have feared for you

I give freely of what is mine to give
Yet you take more than I am able

You hurt me more and more
You ignore my pain and my cries

I am ancient, but I am not immortal
I have a time, why do you seek to rob me of it

Through the years I have been here
for you and yours

For your grandmothers and their grandmothers
and their grandmothers

I would stay to see your children raise their children
But I cannot, for I am dying   →

I do not measure the passing of time as you do
Nevertheless, I know my time is coming
and it is soon

I love you my children, but I fear I will fail you
And even though, you have failed me first

Anger is not in me, for I was created of love,
as were you
Therefore, the toughest part of goodbye

Is knowing that you cannot go on without me
That your time will end, far too soon
and no one will know

This great journey this grand adventure
called humanity
Will be undone as if it never existed

I will care for you as long as I am able
Yet when the rivers no longer flow,
when the trees die

When the wind rages and the storms come
Know that it is not my anger
it is the end of the love

The love I can no longer give,
the love you can no longer take

It is my end, and sadly, it is yours
I love you my children
but I fear I will fail you

And even though you have failed me first
Anger is not in me, for I was created of love,
as were you

Therefore, the toughest part of goodbye
Is knowing that you cannot go on without me
That your time will end,
far too soon and no one will know

This great journey this grand adventure
called humanity
Will be undone as if it never existed

I will care for you as long as I am able
Yet when the rivers no longer flow,
when the trees die

When the wind rages and the storms come
Know that it is not my anger
it is the end of the love

The love I can no longer give,
the love you can no longer take
It is my end, and sadly, it is yours.

Climate Change?

The truth of the land is a long and difficult journey,
but it is past time it was told
The land needs a voice, for though
she speaks, we do not listen
We need to remember our creation and hers
and the link that exists
A link that was forged when your ancestors
first placed foot upon her
It is a link that cannot be broken,
no matter the time or generations that pass
Whether it is a living, breathing connection
and part of your daily life
Or if it exists buried behind walls of apathy,
greed or ignorance it is still there
It can be celebrated, or it can remain hidden
behind self-delusion
But it can never be disconnected
So listen, learn, understand our Mother the Earth
and then maybe we can give her voice
If not, we doom our children to chaos
We do the one thing that every parent swears
upon the birth of their child
They will never do

Take away their right to a future

We as parents swear a silent oath that
we will give our life to protect our children

Yet we are all culpable

I do not have the answers,
for they require more than I

Perhaps I can offer a place to begin

Instead of thinking that climate change
is a problem to be solved

Think instead of Mother Earth
as a soul to be saved

If we can do this simple thing
we can change everything.

It Is Time

She is beauty, she is life and she is spirit

It is time to stand, to stand together

It is time to ensure our children have a future

It is time to offer our prayers and ceremonies,
our protection

It is time to show the world

That the people of the land
understand, respect and protect
the fundamental principles of life

It is time to remember the water

It is time to remember our duty
to our Mother the Earth

It is time.

Justice is Blind

Justice must not be confined by the walls
that make up the rules and regulations
Justice is a living, breathing thing of
morale and spirit

Justice does not always reside here in the brain
Sometimes it resides here in the heart

We will struggle with justice all our lives
Those who seek to categorize
will struggle the most

The world that regulates society
that defines societal norms
Will struggle with this concept, this ideology

Because it seeks to imprison and categorize
Something that cannot be imprisoned
nor solely logically defined

Justice is not blind, it is all encompassing
The rules that seek to define justice may be blind,
but we are not

We want comfort, we want right and wrong
We want black and white
Yet that is seldom where true justice resides.

Who I Am

It can be buried, it can be hidden
I may even be the one hiding it

But who I am can never be lost
Who I am can never be stolen

You can take my culture, deny me my language
Push me from the land

Dress me up as you
Force me to speak your tongue

Beat the Indian out of me
Force me to bend knee in church

But who I am can never be lost or stolen
My ancestors see me, protect me

Call to me, remember who you are
Remember why you are

Reclaim the tools of our people
Walk in pride no matter
the circumstance of your life

We see you for who you are
And you can never be someone you are not

Pretend if you must, yet no hand,
no fist, no gun, no weapon
Can ever unmake you!

So, I pick up my drum, practice my language
Reclaim that what assists me

Yet it doesn't matter what I wear
Where in life I walk or where I live

For who I am, is always who I am
You can deny me my people, even end my life

Yet when I leave this world
Who I am, goes with me

And I and those who have gone before me
will watch over you

Because who I am, who we are
is who you are.

Masks

I am sorry

I married and tried to live a normal life
It must have been and probably still is
a challenge for those who do and have loved me

I have never been able to find any happiness
in this world
I have had many pleasurable and
wonderful moments
But I have never been able to stay in those moments

I love my family and friends, I do
But I cannot free my thoughts
from the passing of time,
the futility of our existence
Moments even great ones amount to nothing

Part of a cog that turns and the machine moves on
The cog breaks, replace it and move on
I have always felt this, thought this way,
my entire life

I have searched for answers in the physical,
spiritual, and even the
addictions this reality has to offer

No matter the answers,
I find I cannot hold them very long

It made it very difficult to maintain
real relationships

All my life I have been alone

Do not get me wrong, no one wears
the masks better than me

I can become anybody, anything
to meet the moment

and I can shine and embrace that reality

But, they are masks and try as we may

We, or at least I, cannot keep the masks on forever

I wish I could find happiness
on the surface of the world

But it has denied me

I escape in so many ways
But I am always caught and dragged back.

Live

I will leave you some day, it may be in years
or it may be tomorrow

I will not wish it, and I will hold onto every breath,
every sight, and every sound

But my wishes and yours cannot change the passage
of time, nor the frailty of our species

We are born to die, to struggle, to learn, to laugh,
to cry and to love

It is the knowledge that we carry,
some of us fear it, others do not

Of all the things in life we lose in death it is you
the people we must leave behind
that hurts the most

It is not the thought of missing you,
for we will be beyond such things

It is the thought of the pain
we will leave in our wake

We love you and wish that we
could take your pain

For our life will end but you will
carry our memory forever

I will not tell you to dry your eyes and be strong
for there is no shame in tears

A lost love is worth a river of tears

Know that I do not hurt, know that I love you

The first moment I saw you,
I was filled with love
and the last breath I took held your memory

I am not nor was I perfect
I made many mistakes, but I did my best

All I ask of you is the same

Be well, live, love, laugh, be you

For you are what I loved
what touched my heart

You were always enough, just as you are

I am gone, it hurts and that's okay

I have one wish.
Live.
I did.

Humans are Funny

We listen with our ears or see with our eyes

and sometimes we feel with our hearts

rarely do we ever see the world
in its entirety

I have come to realize
we do this so we can protect ourselves,

this is our defence mechanism

So we can continue the story
the story we want to be in

The story we want to hear, see, or feel

It doesn't matter if it's the real story
it's our story and that makes it true

But life and love were not meant to be determined
by what you see

or what you hear, or what you feel

Life and love can only really be experienced
by using all of our gifts equally

If you want to keep your fantasy alive

I do not judge you, nor blame you
for the world is a scary place

and seeing the world as you wish it,

can provide feelings of safety and contentment

It may not be the way we were intended to walk
through this world

but it will get you to the end

I do wonder though, at what cost?

Love

Its not all hand holding and stolen kisses
Its not all meaningful glances
It always starts out that way
But life is full of challenges
And humans are impractical and unpredictable
Each of us comes with our own baggage
our own imperfections
We exist with a myriad of emotions
just yearning to be released
Sometimes we act and then think
Sometimes its harsh words
Sometimes there are tears and hurt
Missed chances and regretted action
Love is not a game to be won
nor a promise of perfection
Love is a journey and within that journey
Everyone will be tested to their limits
There will be pain and loss, tears and heartbreak
Yet there will always be love
A love that is shared with each other
With the children, parents, families and friends

It may retreat further into your heart at times

So it is not always bubbling up
on the surface for the world to see

But it does not leave, it cannot escape,
nor does it really wish to

When we look back
and see the lives we left behind

We will see the good and the bad

We will see the love

We will see the hurt and the pain

And as you reflect, you will notice
someone was always by your side

Holding your hand, kissing you
telling you how much they care

Telling you it will be okay

Only at the end in reflection do you realize that you
could see all this in the eyes of your partner from
the moment you met

Your journey began and ended
the day you fell in love

Life was just catching up.

⤙⟨⟩⤚

*I officiated a wedding for my cousin Jay and his bride
Amanda this poem became my gift.*

Happy Mother's Day

To my grandmother who took me in

To my mom who I miss everyday

To all my crazy aunts

To my sister who always gives good advice
whether I want it or not

To my wife who puts up with me and the kids

To the grumpy clerk and the frustrated customer

To the woman who does it alone

To every woman on this Earth and those who can
only look in from time to time

To the planet herself

Happy Mother's day

Chi-miigwech.

Humanity

It is weird, I always saw my children as my children
I never saw them as the adults they became
Never saw them aging
Or in any physical distress
Pains and hurt I knew were just a part of life
Something they had to pass through
Then one was taken from me
How could this be?
They are my children
How can they be gone when I am here
It is not natural and it is unbelievable
Reality punched me right in the face
My child has died
I cry every day
I wish I would have seen them in reality
Instead of the fantasy my mind created
Maybe it wouldn't have changed anything
But maybe the shock of their humanity
Wouldn't have been so harsh.

Shadows

I hope and I pray that the shadow that
dances across my soul

and covets my spirit will leave me

Yet the pain and the hurt do not lessen

Yesterday the sun shined the birds sang
and I had hope

The pain stopped to watch the birds sing
and the sunshine

It was only a moment, but I thought I hoped that
maybe this was a precursor to better things

Yet the pain and hurt resumed
as if the moment had never occurred

The next day, month, year I saw someone who really
saw me, someone who recognized my pain
so I had hope.

Maybe they could be my salvation
but they were not, so I prayed

And one day, there was a moment when the pain
and hurt were gone, but only for that moment, but
still it gave me hope

All my life I hoped and prayed for
an end to the pain and hurt

Always thinking tomorrow, tomorrow

Until I looked in the mirror and saw that time had
brought a new friend along with the pain and hurt

I realized that my hope and my prayers had helped
to keep me a prisoner all my life

I shall leave this world having never been free

As I shut my eyes for the final time I have
realization, I also have hope

So for a final time I pray.

Spirit Bear

I am a symbol, nothing more

I represent determination, love, pain and hope

I represent the voice of a generation

I am an image for equality, an image for unity

A symbol for reconciliation, perhaps

When I say symbol, do not mistake

A symbol has the power to change the world

People have rallied behind symbols
since time began

A staff, a flag, an idea, a vision

I am a symbol and my strength is your strength

My spirit is your spirit

And if history has taught us anything

It is that your strength is limitless
and your spirit unbreakable

I may be just a symbol, but I am a symbol of
resilience that knows no bounds

For I am your symbol

I am Spirit Bear.

I Am Home

I have always felt the call of the water

In this moment the water is still

I dance along the shore

An eagle circles overhead

The image reflected back
from the water is very beautiful

Yet I am unsure if it is my reflection
or that of the eagle

The moment is so peaceful

I realize that the reflection is all

The eagle, the water and me

Captured in this perfect moment

The spirit, the soul, the heart

The three of us are one

As it was meant to be

As it has always been

I am home.

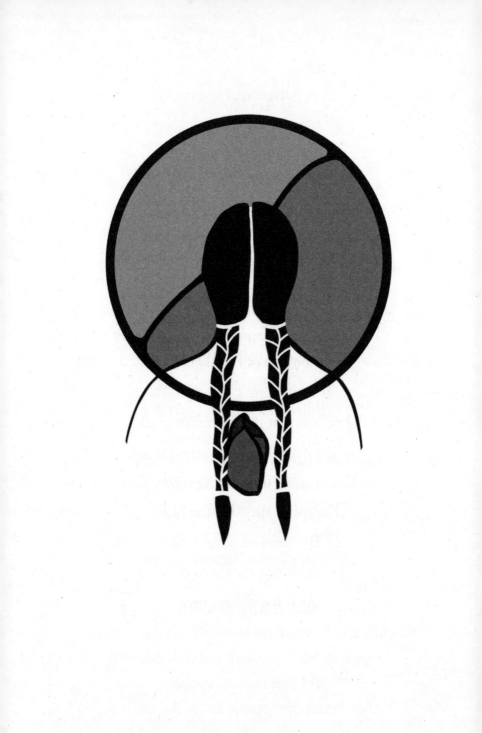

A Broken Heart

My heart will break one day
From the life that I have led
From the things that I have seen
From the stories that I have heard
And from the pain that I have felt

It is sad that those who love me will find me
It will hurt them and I am sorry for that
The doctors will say he died of this or he died of that
But don't you believe it
I died of a broken heart

Too many of our children suffer
Too many children die
Too many people hurt
Too many are gone too soon
And we cannot help but grieve

Call it what you will
Suicide, accident, self-medication, personal neglect
Whatever label society is comfortable with
Yet that does not wash
My family, my people know the truth   →

Whatever reason they ascribe to my passing
I want you to know that at its core
The reason I passed
Was a broken heart
A heart that loves and does not know
how to turn away

I will not be surprised when the end comes
I expect it, for I am flesh and flesh has limits
Death will not stop the grief
As long as the sun rises and the rivers flow
we will grieve
As long as our people hurt, as long as
our children suffer, we will cry

We do not kill ourselves
We do not die by accident
We do not die from self-medication
True these are the labels
But this is the truth

We die from a broken heart.

Smile

A smile is not just a curling of the mouth
or showing of teeth

A smile is contagious, touching everything
the eyes, the face, the spirit

It is a welcome, and an introduction
it says let's be friends

It says I love you, I am glad you are in my life
it says I am here if you need me

A smile lightens every heart, it may be only a little
or only for a moment

Yet in the second that it takes to smile
all the pain and hurt are gone

It is at once the most gregarious greeting
brightening the darkest moments

Yes, it can hide some painful secrets

Yet, whether it hides a tear of sadness or is a
reflection of joy, a smile is a gift to the world

For a smile is not just a moment of happiness
or a reflection of sadness

It is a sharing of soul, the giving of spirit, and that is
the greatest gift one person can give to another

A smile can change the world make it a better place
for a moment, a day, a year

So smile.

Awake

I wake from a night of restless sleep
Dreams are at best bizarre and at worst terrifying
I do not want to rise but I force myself every day
For there are those I love who need me still
I wonder how long that will be enough
And I am so grateful to them
For it is because of them that I have experienced
what has come, why I am here
My days are unchanging
no matter what changes
Moments of relief come only
in precious seconds of distraction
I never sit, I always stand, I fidget,
I walk, I talk, I think, I imagine
Sometimes when no one is there, I cry
Sometimes hard, sometimes soft
most times I don't even know why
At the end of the day I reach for
a drink or two or three
Just enough to make me forget
so I can fall asleep and begin again

I go through all the motions,
you will never see from the outside

To you my world looks bright
and the sun shines on me and mine

But I have never been able to crawl out
from my past, from the dark

Never been able to claim that light, that sun

The sky is never so dark as when you look
through eyes shaded by your past

The world is never so dim as a mind that will not
cannot forget or forgive

I will wake, I will live until I cannot anymore

I say this to you though it will not do any good

This is my tragedy, it is not yours

I own this wholly, it is mine

Do not blame yourself

For you are what made it possible
for me to go so far

Maybe not into the light

But at times because of you
I danced around the edges.

The next poem was written for
my grandchildren's other grandfather Don.
I stole a few lines from myself because
I believe they were appropriate for him.

Another Journey

I leave you today and begin another journey

I do not wish it, and I held on to every breath,
every sight, and every sound

But my wishes and yours cannot change the passage
of time, nor the frailty of the flesh

We are born to die, to struggle, to learn,
to laugh, to cry and to love

I have never wondered how the world saw me

Truth to tell I never really cared

I was, I am content in my reality

The way I lived, the life I lived
has always been enough

Still, as the flesh fails the spirit, I do wonder
Did I show you enough, did you understand me
Although obvious to me and I thought to you
Was it obvious to the world? I love you!

Whether it was Christmas, birthdays
or just Tuesday
My love was and is far beyond
the boundaries of humanity
Maybe my gruff exterior confused others, but to
those who shared my life, I know you knew
How could you not, it filled me and was a part
of everything I felt, everything I did

My family and friends, if there was doubt, let it end
You made my world so much better
by your presence
To my girls, life would not have been
if you had not have been
To my grandchildren, who did, do and
always will own my heart. Hugs and kisses →

I will not tell you to dry your eyes and
be strong, for there is no shame in crying

A lost love is worth a river of tears

The first moment I saw you, I was filled with love
and the last breath I took held your memory

I am not, nor was I perfect, I made mistakes
but I did my best, all I ask of you is the same

I will be watching, do well, live, love, laugh, be you

For you are what I loved
what touched my heart, my soul

You were always enough, just as you are

I have one wish, be honest, be you
chase your dreams

And remember the man who played
a small part in shaping your life.

Patience

It is not patience
it manifests as such to world

But it is the understanding that
all things move and evolve at
societal/community/group pace

and though we yearn and
scream inside for more

We understand that expressing
that frustration
is contrary
to the very change we are
striving to make.

Love

You know I love you

It's been said, it's been believed

It's been echoed

But you will never ever know how much
my heart screams

You will never know how much I love you

Maybe I was wrong and didn't show you

Maybe my own pain was in the way

But I want you to know

I need you to know

That I love you

And I love you is too small

I love you more than you could imagine

More than you could ever dream possible

Someday, you will feel this, you will know this

And I am so happy that you will find it

I just wish I was better at telling, showing

My soul loves you, my heart breaks,
my love is yours

You make me so proud
just by being in the room

My only regret in life is that I have not
done enough

Enough to express the depth of my love

You hear my words

But you don't hear my heart

If only you could see my soul.

Beast

A thin piece of plexiglass and behind this glass is
an angry, sad, vicious creature

who continually leaps, pounds and rages against the glass

And the glass although strong begins to fray
and cracks appear

People come, smile and wave at the plexiglass, they talk
and commiserate and walk away

And the beast is a little confused, but seems
almost happy in the moment

And more people come and they touch and hug the glass
and the beast is quieted
and sleep comes

The sleep is not peaceful but it does last

Hours, days, weeks can pass but eventually the beast rises
and crashes against the glass and it weakens
and begins to splinter

The scenario plays over and over again

However, it is only time we wait on, for although the
crashing is not continuous the glass is never repaired
and the beast never tamed

The question is not if the beast is free it is when and what

For once the glass is down and the creature is free
what does it do?

What do you do?

My Belief

Never stop believing

I used to believe in Santa Claus

Oh, on some levels, I knew it to be unrealistic

But I wanted to believe, long after the
believing had stopped

Yet I knew, that I would be ridiculed, laughed at

My belief was pushed so far down

That I could never recover it, no matter my hopes

Santa may be a myth, but sometimes I think so too
is inclusivity, so is peace, so is love

They all require faith and the ability
to stand against adversity

They all require bravery and heart

It is true, we are stronger in our beliefs
when we believe together

But before that, we must have the courage
to believe by ourselves

Because I cannot become we
until I become me

Never stop believing.

Hurricane or Just Wind

The world tests us

At least we perceive it as such

Racism rears its ugly head, once more

Violence erupts across the lands

People are polarized by perceived corruptness

Many take to the street in defence of their beliefs

Conflict and adversity become a way of life

And so many are swept up along in the wake

It is akin to being caught in the winds of a hurricane

Yet a hurricane allows no independence

Once you are in the midst

You are a part of the hurricane

Seeking sustenance to continue to live

As more and more are embraced
by the strength of the wind

Independence is gone.

Life

What does it mean to live

Is it enough to get up, go to work, propagate,
impart values and die

I find comfort absorbed in the moments of life

So much to do, so much to accomplish

Yet the down times, which I admit are few

Are the most difficult

For they test the faith of anyone

An idle mind may be the devil's playground

But an idle mind is also when we explore
the thoughts we keep at bay

The wisdom of our lives, the decisions we make,
the lives we live, the paths we take

The reflection of the universe, the purpose in
50 60 70 80 90 even 100 brief years in this reality

Are we meant to toil, to ignore the questions that
philosophers, poets and scientists explore?

I think not, I think it is knowledge we must all seek

For it is not something we can ask others to teach us

For it is unique

And though we are all connected

We are still individuals.

Birth Day

The potential you have when you
come into this world is endless

The love and affection that greets you, overpowering

And every year you get to renew this moment

The path in life is challenging, hurtful and painful

Yet it is mixed with joy and pleasure

Such is our journey through this world

Regardless of the trials you faced or the moments
you enjoyed

This is your renewal, a reminder

That your potential is unlimited and again you are
surrounded by love

As the years pass

We forget and this day becomes just another day

But that is a mistake, and we do an injustice

To the love and the potential
that came to this world

To the day your spirit began this journey

Your birthday should always be a renewal
a celebration of creation

A thank you
to Creator for the breath of life

A thank you to
your ancestors for this journey

And a thank you from us
for the gift of you.

Honour

No words do I have to describe you
Nor do I need any
It is true some people need to be described
Others desperately need to be understood
You my friend do not

Your deeds and actions transcend words
and defy description
You are a person of immense honour and integrity
But you are far more than that
You prove it daily by simply being you
And in your case, that's more than enough

We greet you always with love and respect
And wherever you walk in life it will remain so
There are many words to describe you
To show respect and honour
The one I choose to use most often is friend.

I See You

I can see you as who you are
Not as I wish you are
Not as I pretend you are
Not as the world thinks you are
I see you as just who you are

A girl, a woman, a mother
Perfect, no
Perfect for us, yes
I accept and appreciate you
Just as you are

So my gift does not come in a bag
Nor does it go in a vase
My gift is a happy smile, a loving look
And the knowledge that you are loved
For just who you are.

Always Observed

Why can we not disagree
without attacking?

Why can we not have a difference
of opinion without hating?

Do we not realize that our children see us
our grandchildren hear us

They love us and want to be us

Do we want them to be us?

To carry this generational trauma
for another generation

We have a right to the anger
but we must try and understand
where it comes from

or we will never heal
nor will our children

Do we not want it to end?

If not for ourselves at least for them

Let them walk in the light

Do not be the one
who holds them in the dark

Do not make them carry the pain
and hurt of the past into their future

and their children's future

It's time to stop this continual walk
in pain and anger

time to stop hurting each other

It is time to be better

Once long ago we were

For our children

We must be again.

The Clock Ticks On

I sit alone in the dark, warmed by the fire, lost in
contemplation, barely aware of an old clock ticking.
The end creeps upon me as night steals away the day.
I measure time in hours; not days, not months,
but hours, perhaps moments.
I have said my goodbyes, kissed my last kiss.
And in these final moments, I wonder, not the magic
wonder of the young who feel invincible and have so
many dreams. But the wonders of a long life that is
ending like the final chapter of a story.
I enjoyed the book. I remember the good, the bad and
the ugly. Like all good books that come to an end, the
finale is never the finale.
We always consider the characters and where they
journey once the pen is finished.
Do we have a continuing tale once this book called
life closes? I hope so, I have prayed so. But even
though I carried beliefs and values all my life to this
moment, for the end of my story, now that it is here,
I wonder.
I also wonder how the world will remember me
if they do remember me.
I spent a lot of time in the moment
because that was my role.

I strove to do good when I could but inside my role.

The world has a short memory and a narrow one.

All my good could be overshadowed by one moment and not even a moment I wanted.

Because we are seldom judged by our desire, it is always the outcome. And once started down a path, that desire, that story has a life of its own and an ending I could not imagine, for others will become part of that story, many hands will play a role.

So, will I have a place in history? Maybe! Will it be a positive one? Who knows, for judgement continues long after life ends.

I suppose it really doesn't matter, for I will be gone one way or another.

Life is so short, and I am not sure whether it was better to live in the moment or make grandiose plans for the future. All my thoughts and musings seem so irrelevant.

Did I spend enough time with my family and friends? Sadly, in this moment, that too doesn't matter.

I guess the only question that matters at this moment:

Was I the hero in my own story?

A smile crosses my face, my heart beats its last and the clock ticks on.

a little bit of hope

Tragedies are part of our life

They change us

But they do not define us

Our journey continues with the gifts
we have been given

and with the trials we have faced

We move forward, that's humanity

We don't always do it smiling and laughing

Sometimes we do it cowering or crying

But we do it

The world may crumble around us

But we will always try

We will always have hope

It is in our DNA

We may stutter and stall

Yet we find a way

Push, pull, find a hill, or ask for help

We move forward

We all need inspiration at times

It is not hard to find

Just breathe deep and remember

Your family, your friends

The Children

The ancestors who never gave up

Even if it appears hopeless

We do not quit!

The Prince of New Credit (A Bonus)

The following are three true stories of the Prince of New Credit. The first one told by his cousin and the second told by one of his best friends, the last one told by me as the person, his aunt Julie, has since passed away. The Prince is also known as Gilbert, Gil, Gilly, Stacey, Stace and very rarely by a select few, little Stace.

～◦～

Gilbert's girlfriend wanted to go look at apartments in Brantford, something that Gilbert didn't want to do. He didn't like the area and didn't want to live in Brantford. He was sitting in the car when she went in to check out a potential apartment. While sitting there, he looked in the rear-view mirror and noticed someone who looked like they were in their early 20s. The man was holding a knife to two kids who looked to be in their early teens. Some people may have just pretended they didn't see what was going on, but not Gil. Gilbert wasn't sure what was going on, but got out of his car anyway. He walked right over to the individual holding the knife. The man must have realized that Gilbert was not there to make friends. The knife wielding man said, "I don't have any problems with you, man."

Gilbert grabbed the man by his wrist and shirt, and slammed him on the ground. While holding the man's wrist, he slammed his hand against the sidewalk. The man released the knife, Gil stood up, and the man ran off. The kids looked at Gil and said, "Thank you sir." Gil told them to go home. Gil hated bullies.

The second true story involves the Prince and his buddy who was on a first date with his now wife.

✂〜{}〜✂

Jesse spent time in a bar in Port Dover and had met a beautiful young woman who he wanted to date. He finally got the nerve up to ask her out after talking to her a few times in the bar as a customer. He decided that it would be good to take Gilly as backup to his date, I don't know why.

They arrive at the bar. Jesse goes in and the Prince goes in separate and sits away from Jesse as he does not want to intrude on the first date. Things are progressing well for Jesse and his wife to be, when all of a sudden the Prince, who is a large and intimidating man, comes running up from the back of the bar, scoops up Jesse's date in his arms, and runs out of the building. She, not knowing who the Prince is, begins screaming and asking for help, trying to hold onto the door frame as the Prince carries her out. Once outside he sets her down and says hi I am Gil, Jessies friend and by this time Jesse arrives, laughing and reintroduces them and explains the whole tale to his future bride.

The third true story involves the Prince and his aversion to the police. As a First Nation person I totally understand this reluctance to sometimes interact with the police. He was always worried that the police would accost him and I saw it in action one time—that story is about the Prince and two women. But that is another story for another time. Knowing the Prince, maybe he had a particular reason for avoiding the police. Anyway, the Prince asked his aunt Julie, who was across the street from where he lived, if she would keep an eye out and let him know if the popo were around. Julie said how can I do that you just said that you broke your phone. How am I to tell you if I see the police? He said well since you're across the street from me, just stick your head out the door or the window and let me know if the coast is clear. If it's clear just yell Caw Caw, Caw Caw!

There are many more stories of the Prince of New Credit not all suitable for a G-rated tale, and some difficult to tell without incriminating others. One story involves hundreds of people and an almost-gang fight that eventually was turned into a song by a local band. That's for another day, perhaps another book?

Miigwech,

Giima Laforme

Afterword, Glimmers

⚘

YOU MAY KNOW HIM as Chief Laforme, Giima, Stace, Ralph, husband, dad, uncle, friend, councillor, cousin. He is a lot of different things to a lot of different people. When I look back at this man of many names and hats I remember snippets of time.

As a young child, he was a protector—big, strong, and steady. He was the one who lifted us up, dangling from his bicep, on his back while he did push ups, or drove us to buy school clothes, or to school with his head out of the window because the wipers were broken.

As a teen, he was funny, teasing, always around. When he moved out from next door, his family breaking up, our collective hearts were broken. Where was he going? Not far and not for long. We were too young to understand, but happy he was still nearby, lifting weights, pull ups, Johnny Bravo triangle-shaped. Consistent.

As a young adult, he was a guide, still funny, still teasing; finding love again and remarrying, adding to the family. His door was always open, and upon entering, whether hungry or not he would make you something to eat. An offering of whatever he had, was yours because that's how he showed he cared. He had the gravitational pull to keep family coming together. Breakfast, Christmas, barbecue, random Tuesdays. Always up for a chat or debate, he encouraged everyone to seek more, or learn and do more.

Once when I was frustrated with the state of Indigenous politics, he told me, "You must have hope. Find a way."

As a grown up he has helped me through my own grief and pain, guiding me personally and professionally. He remains strong and steady. I see him in a new way. Over the years, I didn't realize that I was not only losing members of my own family, my grandparents, father, aunt, cousin. I was also watching him slowly lose his family, watched him grieve, but still supporting others, showing up consistently for everyone else and eventually laughing again. What makes him keep hope alive after everything he's been through? I don't know. I may never know, I've only known him my whole life, not his. Those who have known him for his entire life, I count as lucky. But what I do know is he is someone who wants to do good, always wanting to help, even when he is hurting, when he is questioned, and called down but how?

Maybe because he is able to see the glimmers—glimmers of hope, glimmers of love in this world that if you're not paying attention to, you'll miss. Glimmers are the opposite of triggers. Life is full of love and loss, but never absent of grief. And through it all, he remains observant to this world around him. He is not blind to hardship and never saved from it. But rather he sees the hope everywhere, and he remains strong, steady—heart and eyes open for what is next. As his ancestors were that came before, he is resilient.

— *Kate Laforme, 2024*

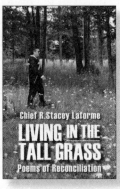

**DURVILE &
UpRoute Books**

OTHER SELECTED TITLES IN THE
SPIRIT OF NATURE SERIES

VISIT DURVILE.COM
OR CLICK THE QR CODE FOR
MORE INFO ON THESE TITLES

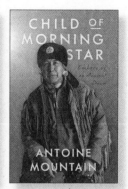

**WHY ARE YOU STILL
HERE?: A LILLIAN MYSTERY**
By Lynda Partridge
ISBN: 9781988824826

**NAHGANNE TALES OF THE
NORTHERN SASQUATCH**
By Red Grossinger
ISBN 9781988824598

**CHILD OF MORNING STAR
EMBERS of an ANCIENT DAWN**
By Antoine Mountain
ISBN: 9781990735103

**MIDNIGHT STORM
MOONLESS SKY**
By Alex Soop
ISBN: 9781990735127

**THE RAINBOW, THE
SONGBIRD & THE MIDWIFE**
By Raymond Yakeleya
ISBN: 9781988824574

**WHISTLE AT NIGHT AND
THEY WILL COME**
By Alex Soop
ISBN: 9781990735301

A percentage of publisher's proceeds and author royalties have been donated to: The Food Bank, Calgary and Bracebridge; Oldman Watershed Council, Stargate Women's Group; CFWEP Clark Fork Watershed Environment Project; Chytomo: Support for Ukrainian Literature and Book Publishers; "Home In Our Hearts" for Ukrainian Evacuees; The Canada Ukraine Foundation; Doctors Without Borders; The Elizabeth Yakeleya Fund; Calgary Communities Against Sexual Abuse; The Canadian Women's Foundation; The Salvation Army; (MMIWG) Missing and Murdered Indigenous Women and Girls; Days for Girls International; Red Door Family Shelter, Toronto; Ikwe-Widdjiitiwin Family Shelter, Winnipeg; The Schizophrenia Society of Canada; and the Elizabeth Fry Society.

About Chief Stacey Laforme

STACEY LAFORME was born on a cold December morning into a life of alcoholism and abuse. At fifteen, he left home and lived on the street, eventually finding a home with both of his grandmothers. He started his first job at twelve years old, eventually going into the family business and joining the Ironworkers Union. He retired from iron work and, as he admits, "If I am honest, I was not the best at iron work." He attended college late in life. After his mother passed away at the age of fifty, he was elected to council. He ran and was elected Chief of the Mississaugas of the Anishinaabe in December 2015, a few months after his father passed away. Chief Laforme says, "I am dedicated to my people, and to all the people who live within our treaty lands." He is an honorary Senior Fellow of Massey College at the University of Toronto, and he recently led a delegation to the UK, Scotland, and the Isle of Man. He was the first Giima (Chief) to meet with the British Monarch in over 160 years.